GREAT AMERICAN MEMORIALS

A DATE WITH DESTINY

The WOMEN IN MILITARY
SERVICE FOR AMERICA
MEMORIAL

Brent Ashabranner

Photographs by Jennifer Ashabranner

Twenty-First Century Books
Brookfield, Connecticut

Published by Twenty-First Century Books
a Division of The Millbrook Press, Inc.
2 Old New Milford Road
Brookfield, Connecticut 06804

Visit us at our Web site: http://www.millbrookpress.com

Library of Congress Cataloging-in-Publication Data
Ashabranner, Brent K., 1921–
A date with destiny: the Women in Military Service
for America Memorial/Brent Ashabranner;
photographs by Jennifer Ashabranner.
p.   cm.
Includes bibliographical references and index.
Summary: Describes the planning and creation of the
Women in Military Service for America Memorial, profiles
some of the servicewomen involved, and presents a general
history of women in military service.
ISBN 0–7613–1472–5 (lib. bdg.)
1. Women in Military Service for America Memorial (Arlington, Va.)
Juvenile literature.   [1. Women in Military Service for America Memorial
(Arlington, Va.)   2. National monuments.   3. Women and the
military—History.   4. United States—Armed Forces—Women—History.]
I. Ashabranner, Jennifer, ill.   II. Title.
UB418.W65A85   2000
355.1'6—dc21   99-36384   CIP

Contents

You have taken off silk
and put on khaki. . . .
You have a debt and a date.
A debt to democracy,
a date with destiny.

—OVETA CULP HOBBY,
COLONEL, Director of Women's
Army Corps, World War II, addressing
a group of Women's Army Corps
officers beginning training

Author's NOTE

Many people helped Jennifer and me gather the material and take the photographs for this book, and we thank all of them. I would particularly like to thank Brigadier General Wilma L. Vaught, USAF Retired, President of the Women's Memorial Foundation, and Dr. Judith Bellafaire, Curator of the Women's Memorial. Both General Vaught and Dr. Bellafaire gave generously of their time to provide me with information and invaluable advice. I also wish to thank Ms. F. G. Shutsy-Reynolds, a former member of the Women's Airforce Service Pilots (WASP) program, for her personal insights into that remarkable organization.

One explanation about names may be needed. Women in Military Service for America Memorial is the official name of the memorial that is the subject of this book. Because of the length of the name, however, the board of directors of the memorial gave its approval for the use of the shorter name, the Women's Memorial, when that use is appropriate. I, therefore, have used the two names interchangeably.

—*Brent Ashabranner*

FOUR SETS OF STAIRS *leading to an upper terrace of the new Women's Memorial were cut through the original hemicycle wall. A brick courtyard, named the Court of Valor, was built in front of the reflecting pool. Colorado and Vermont marble was used in refurbishing the hemicycle.*

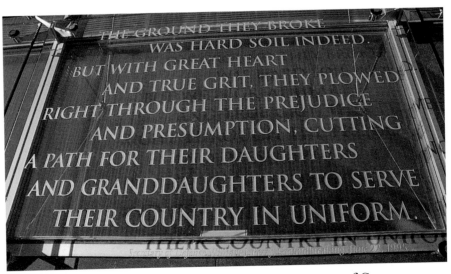

THE GROUND THEY BROKE WAS HARD SOIL INDEED. BUT WITH GREAT HEART AND TRUE GRIT, THEY PLOWED RIGHT THROUGH THE PREJUDICE AND PRESUMPTION, CUTTING A PATH FOR THEIR DAUGHTERS AND GRANDDAUGHTERS TO SERVE THEIR COUNTRY IN UNIFORM.

A QUOTATION FROM THE ADDRESS *of Secretary of Defense William J. Perry at the memorial's groundbreaking ceremony is etched on one of the terrace skylights.*

One

VETERANS DAY

On a cool, bright day in November, Veterans Day, Jennifer and I went once more to the Women in Military Service for America Memorial. This setting for the memorial, at the entrance to Arlington National Cemetery, could not be more dramatic or more surrounded by American history. On a straight line, or axis, in front of the memorial, across the Potomac River, is one of our nation's most cherished shrines, the Lincoln Memorial. On a hill just above the Women's Memorial is the grave of President John F. Kennedy, with its eternal flame.

Still on a straight line above the Women's Memorial stands Arlington House, once the home of General Robert E. Lee. The great house commands the highest hill and appears to be watching over the cemetery, as if protecting it. Now it watches over the Women's Memorial, not officially a part of the cemetery but seemingly so as it sits nestled against this hallowed ground.

7

A VIEW OF THE LINCOLN MEMORIAL *from the upper terrace of the Women's Memorial. Memorial Bridge, which links Arlington National Cemetery and the Lincoln Memorial, is symbolic of the reuniting of the North and South after the Civil War.*

Jennifer and I have been to the Women's Memorial many times, but as I walked toward it today I had the same feeling that I had had the first time I visited it: a feeling of discovery. For if you did not know the memorial was there, behind the gray stone ceremonial entrance wall, you would have to wander into it by chance. There is no directional sign to guide you, and there is no visible structure that you can recognize as a building. The memorial is just there, a place of quiet beauty, dug out of the earth and stone of a hill behind the gateway wall.

The Women in Military Service for America Memorial, opened to the public in October 1997, is the newest memorial in the great monumental corridor of Washington, D.C. The corridor begins with the National Capitol Building, ends with Arlington House, and includes such American treasures as the Lincoln Memorial, the Washington Monument, the Vietnam Veterans Memorial, the Smithsonian Institution, and the National Art Gallery.

Dedicated to honoring the almost two million women who have served and are now serving in the American military from the founding of the nation to the present, the Women's Memorial fits confidently and securely into the monumental corridor of our national capital.

Over four million people visit Arlington National Cemetery every year, and many thousands of them come on Veterans Day. On this day a steady flow of visitors came to the Women's Memorial, some clearly finding it by accident as they made their way to other destinations in the cemetery. I can almost always tell when people are seeing the Women's Memorial for the first time. Their expression as they enter through the heavy glass doors is one of surprise, almost of awe.

Since from the outside there is no indication of anything behind the ceremonial wall, they are not prepared for what they see: a beautifully lit 33,000-square-foot (3,066-square-meter) building that combines an exhibit gallery, a computer register room, a Hall of Honor, and a 196-seat theater where films about women in America's military history are shown. All the rooms, exhibit alcoves, and passageways conform gracefully to the semicircular shape of the ceremonial wall. Part of the wonderful light in the memorial comes from 108 skylights on the upper terrace. Quotations by or about women who have served in the military are etched into some of the skylights.

On one of the skylights is a quotation by Clara Barton, the Angel of the Battlefield, who served in two American wars and founded the American Red Cross in 1881:

THE HALL OF HONOR *includes the United States flag, the flags of the fifty states, the District of Columbia flag, and those of all U.S. territories. The large block of Colorado Yule marble at the end of the room is the "sister block" of marble to that used in Arlington National Cemetery's Tomb of the Unknowns. The Hall of Honor contains a book that lists the names of all the women who have been killed in action or were prisoners of war.*

THERE ARE 108 SKYLIGHTS *that make the Women's Memorial a place of warm, natural light.*

From the storm-splashed decks of the *Mayflower* . . . to the present hour, woman has stood like a rock for the welfare and glory of the country, and one might add . . . unwritten, unrewarded, and almost unrecognized.

Now, on the threshold of a new century, the contributions of women to their country's defense are being recognized in the Women in Military Service for America Memorial.

The memorial's exhibit gallery tells the story of that service chronologically from the eighteenth century to the present day. The story is told with pictures, words, and a fascinating collection of reminders of women's military service overseas and on

THE "OVERSEAS WITH THE MILITARY IN WORLD WAR II" EXHIBIT *tells a stirring story of women determined to serve their country in a time of crisis.*

the home front: a telegram ordering a Women's Army Corps (WAC) recruit to basic training in World War II, notes taken by trainees on how to repair guns and pack parachutes, the uniform of a navy nurse who was captured on Guam in World War II, "mosquito boots" worn by army nurses in Africa in 1942. The photographs tell their own special story—the "Hello Girls" of World War I, bilingual Signal Corps telephone operators sent to France to help military communications between Americans and French; a woman in a LINK trainer teaching a man how to shoot at a moving target; four Red Cross nurses whose ship was torpedoed off Greenland in 1941.

On this Veterans Day many of the memorial visitors were older women, and I overheard two talking about the mosquito boots in the Overseas With the Military in World War II exhibit.

"I could give them my old army shoes," one of the women said.

"You were a nurse?" the other woman asked.

"WAC," said the first woman. "Stationed on New Guinea. There were insects of every color, shape, and size. They loved shoes. You had to shake them out every morning before you put your shoes on. Some days I thought I was crazy for volunteering."

"But you're glad you did," the other woman stated. It was not a question.

The former WAC nodded. "I've always been glad I was there," she said.

And that, I thought, probably sums up the way most women veterans feel, wherever they served.

The Veterans Day ceremony started in the Court of Valor in front of the memorial at three o'clock. There was a gathering of several hundred, mostly women, many in uniforms of the

U.S. ARMY SERGEANT FIRST CLASS *Marcy Diaz sings the national anthem at the first Women's Memorial Veterans Day ceremony.*

various military branches, but many men, too, and children. Brigadier General Wilma L. Vaught, president of the Women in Military Service for America Memorial Foundation, presided. She noted the importance of this day set aside to honor all veterans, living and dead, who served in the armed forces of the United States. This was the first Veterans Day observance at the Women's Memorial, she pointed out—the first of many to come.

After the presentation of Colors, the invocation, and the national anthem, several women in different branches of the armed forces spoke about what their years of military service had meant to them. Yeoman Second Class Deborah L. Reed of the U.S. Coast Guard received warm applause when General

Vaught told the crowd that she had that very day reenlisted for another six-year tour of duty in the Coast Guard. Yeoman Reed began by sharing that she had joined the Coast Guard because she had wanted a job that made a difference. The thrust of her brief remarks was that freedom is America's heart but could only be won and secured by the courage and sacrifice of the veterans being honored on this day.

When I looked at a biographical note on Yeoman Reed, I noticed that she had a number of varied Coast Guard awards and medals. One was the Coast Guard Humanitarian Service Medal; another was the Coast Guard Rifle Marksmanship ribbon. I am glad she is on our side.

A crowd favorite that day undoubtedly was Gunnery Sergeant Brenda L. Warren of the U.S. Marine Corps. When General Vaught introduced her and gave her the microphone,

U.S. MARINE CORPS GUNNERY SERGEANT
Brenda L. Warren

she prompted, "Take it, Gunny." And Gunny Warren certainly took it.

She had been a good student in high school, Sergeant Warren told the Veterans Day audience, but she didn't want to go to college. She wanted to see the world, and for her that meant joining some branch of the armed services.

"The army recruiter wanted me to run two miles. I said no way. The navy recruiter wanted me to swim. I couldn't even float. The air force recruiter wanted me to aim high. I was afraid of heights. The Marine Corps recruiter, Staff Sergeant Wendall J. Mahatha, wanted me to have fun. I told him to sign me up.

"I would soon learn that a marine's idea of fun was not quite what I expected. In boot camp I had fun running, swimming, and climbing tall objects. I had fun learning to march, walk, crawl, and talk. I learned the meaning of discipline, esprit de corps, and teamwork just to name a few."

But her boot training was cut short when she was thrown from a troop van and hospitalized for most of the second phase of training. When she was released, her arm was in a sling. Even moving was difficult; she could barely dress herself. She was given the option of trying to finish training or starting all over again when she was well. Here is what happened:

"My bunkmate and other recruits said they would help, and they let me stay. I learned the true meaning of teamwork then and there. As members of Platoon 1180 helped me dress and even shower, I learned I could depend on others. At final inspection I received an outstanding—uniforms pressed, boots polished, and my arm still in a sling. I received an outstanding because others were willing to sacrifice and lend a hand even though they had responsibilities of their own. I've carried this memory with me throughout my career, always remembering that no marine succeeds alone. It is truly a team effort."

And Gunny Warren added: "If any of you ever see retired Master Sergeant Wendall J. Mahatha, tell him I'm still having fun."

Later I learned what a serious career professional Gunnery Sergeant Brenda L. Warren is. She has been in Marine Corps service for nineteen years. She has served in Japan and on Okinawa. She has held administrative staff positions at marine stations from California to North Carolina. She is presently administrative assistant with the Defense Advisory Committee on Women in the Services at the Pentagon. And although she said she didn't want to go to college, her record shows that someplace along the way she had acquired an Associate Degree in Business Management from Maria Regina College in Syracuse, New York.

After the Veterans Day ceremony ended, Jennifer and I went back into the memorial where we met Yeoman Reed and her mother, Pamela Bakie. Mrs. Bakie had flown in from New Hampshire to see her daughter reenlist in the Coast Guard and to be with her at the Veterans Day ceremony. Yeoman Reed is on the staff of the Master Chief Petty Officer of the Coast Guard in Washington, D.C. I learned that she is married—her husband is not in the military—with two young sons.

That piece of information reminded me that there was a time less than twenty-five years ago when a woman in the military had to resign if she wanted to raise a family. Now, although her duty assignment may sometimes separate her from her family, she can remain in the service—just as male members of the military have always done.

And the stripes and insignia on the sleeve of Yeoman Second Class Reed's uniform reminded me of another difference between serving in the military today and in the past. On one of the glass skylights on the terrace is etched this statement:

U.S. COAST GUARD YEOMAN SECOND CLASS *Deborah L. Reed and her mother*

"I'm still so proud of my naval service. I would do it all over if I could."

The statement is by Mildred Pearl Lane, who was a yeoman second class during World War I more than eighty years ago. In those days women were accepted into the military only in times of national emergency and were dropped from the service when the emergency ended. Today that has changed.

Women in the military have every right of service continuity that men have. With her new six-year reenlistment Yeoman Reed is going to do it all over.

Two

A GATEWAY TO HISTORY

The idea for a memorial to honor women in military service for America had been around for years, but it did not find a voice until 1982. In that year the American Veterans Committee (AVC) began a campaign to build such a memorial. The AVC, a national organization of veterans of World Wars I and II, the Korean War, and the Vietnam War, spoke with a loud voice, and its message was clear: The largely overlooked and forgotten contributions of women in the military defense of the nation should be recognized and honored.

Women have taken part in every American war since the Revolutionary War. A few stories are well known, such as that of Mary Ludwig Hays McCauley, known to history as "Molly Pitcher," who took her injured husband's place at his cannon in the Battle of Monmouth in 1778. But how well do we know the story of Dr. Mary Edwards Walker, who served as acting assistant surgeon in the Union Army during the Civil War and who is the only woman ever to receive the Medal of Honor,

SCHOOL STUDENTS LEARNING *more about the heroic work of nurses during the Spanish-American War*

our nation's highest military honor? Do we remember the hundreds of army and navy civilian women nurses who served on contract in high-risk hospitals in Cuba during the Spanish-American War, twenty of whom lost their lives? How much do we know today about the 400,000 women who volunteered for the Women's Army Corps during World War II? Many served in every remote geographic location to which American troops were sent. Do we remember that eighty-seven military nurses were prisoners of war in the Pacific and in Europe?

Few people today have any knowledge or understanding of the difficulties faced and the sacrifices made by servicewomen of earlier times who chose to serve their country in any of the military branches. Women served when the kinds of jobs open to them and the chances of promotion were severely limited, when women were not entitled to veterans' benefits that men took for granted. They served when women serving overseas were not provided with legal protection if they were captured by the enemy, when women who died in the line of duty were not entitled to military burial.

Clearly, as the American Veterans Committee strongly contended, America needed a permanent reminder of women's contributions to the nation's defense—to what they have been in the past, what they are now, and what they will be in the future.

But great ideas are not always thought of as great when they are first presented. In truth, they are often met with doubt or ridicule. Although no one ridiculed the idea of a women's military memorial when it was proposed, in the beginning there was little official enthusiasm or support for it. In 1985, Congresswoman Mary Rose Oakar, chairperson of the House Committee on Libraries and Memorials, introduced legislation for a memorial to recognize the contribution of women in military service. A Senate committee initially voted against the proposal, and the Secretary of the Interior and the National Park Service expressed doubts about the proposed memorial. They felt that the monuments and statues being planned at that time—the Vietnam Women's Memorial and the Navy Memorial, which included women—would make another women's military memorial unnecessary.

"We don't need a statue or a monument!"

Those were the words of retired Air Force Brigadier General Wilma L. Vaught, who was destined to become the driving force behind the creation of the Women in Military Service for America Memorial.

What was needed, General Vaught and many others insisted, was a memorial that would make the contributions of American servicewomen, and other women who had worked closely with the military, a visible part of our nation's heritage. It would be a memorial that would inspire other women to follow in their footsteps. The memorial had to be a place where the stories of servicewomen's heroism could be told and where their sheer hard, unglamorous, but necessary work in the military would be made clear.

There followed a vigorous educational and lobbying campaign by the American Veterans Committee, other distinguished women veterans, and even military women on active duty. The AVC established a Women in Military Service for America Memorial Foundation, which would be responsible for creating and building the memorial if approved by Congress.

After careful study the National Capital Memorial Commission voted unanimously in favor of a women's military memorial. The approval of that influential body was critical, and with its positive vote the Secretary of the Interior withdrew his opposition to the memorial. In the late fall of 1986 both the House of Representatives and the Senate passed a bill authorizing the building of a memorial to honor women who have served in the military forces of the United States. The bill specified that the memorial could be built on federal land in or near Washington, D.C., and gave the responsibility for building the memorial to the Women in Military Service for America Memorial Foundation. The bill further stipulated that U.S. government money was not to be used in building the memorial. On November 6, 1986, President Ronald Reagan signed the bill as Public Law 99-610.

Before the end of the year the American Veterans Committee coordinated the creation of a board of directors for the Women in Military Service for America Memorial Foundation. The board was made up of distinguished military and civilian women; General Vaught was elected president of the foundation by the board.

General Vaught proved to be a dynamic, tireless leader. One of the most decorated military women in U.S. history, she is also one of the few to achieve the rank of General. Among

her numerous military decorations are the Air Force Distinguished Service Medal, the Air Force Legion of Merit, the Bronze Star Medal, and the Vietnam Service Medal with four service stars. General Vaught was the first woman to serve with a Strategic Air Command bombardment wing on an operational deployment. Her twenty-eight years of service took her to assignments in Spain, Guam, Vietnam, various U.S. Air Force bases, and the Pentagon. With a Bachelor of Science degree from the University of Illinois and a Master of Business Administration degree from the University of Alabama, General Vaught held positions as a financial comptroller in her various assignments. Her main activity as her career progressed was as a management analyst—she improved military operations. Her last assignment was as

LESS THAN A MILE *from the Women's Memorial, across Memorial Bridge and close by the black granite wall of the Vietnam Veterans Memorial, stands the Vietnam Women's Memorial. It commemorates the contributions of the 11,500 women in uniform who served overseas during the Vietnam War. The work of sculptor Glenna Goodacre, the dark bronze group statue depicts a nurse holding a wounded soldier. Another servicewoman anxiously scans the sky for an evacuation helicopter. A third kneels to pick up the fallen soldier's helmet. At the groundbreaking ceremony for the memorial on July 29, 1993, General Colin Powell, then chairman of the Joint Chiefs of Staff, gave a moving tribute: "The nurses saw the bleakest, most terrifying face of war...the mangled men, the endless sobs of wounded kids...not just now and then, but day after day, night after hellish night." General Powell concluded by saying that the memorial would "celebrate the hope and the strength, the tenderness and the power, the kindness and the passion" of American women who served in Vietnam.*

Commander of the U.S. Military Entrance Processing Command in Chicago. She was responsible for a staff of 3,300 persons, who administered a million entrance tests each year.

From the very beginning of her association with the Women's Memorial, General Vaught viewed the memorial as a gift to the American people and was determined to have it built in a place where the millions of visitors to Washington, D.C., every year could find it easily. The first and most vital task was finding a place: Vaught felt that the site should have some relationship with the military. Even before the memorial could be designed, architects had to know where it would be built.

In the spring of 1988, General Vaught and the foundation committee began their search. Their guide was David Sherman of the National Park Service. General Vaught believed that a site on the National Mall was out of the question. No space was available for the kind of memorial building needed; and even if a place could be found, approval for a Mall location could take years.

But the search for a site was discouraging. Every available location was remote and too far from Washington's major tourist attractions such as the Lincoln Memorial, the Washington Monument, the Vietnam Veterans Memorial, the Air and Space Museum, and other national treasures.

On returning to National Park headquarters at the end of a day of fruitless site searching, the committee drove past the entrance to Arlington National Cemetery, with its 270-foot (82-meter) neoclassical Greek "hemicycle," a semicircular concrete and stone wall. On each side of the wall, which rises to a height of 30 feet (9 meters), stand two large wrought-iron ceremonial gates with roads leading into the cemetery.

As she looked at the entrance wall, General Vaught realized that she knew nothing about it. "I've never understood that thing," she said to David Sherman. "What is it? What does it mean?"

AN AERIAL VIEW OF THE ORIGINAL HEMI-CYCLE *wall at the entrance to Arlington National Cemetery before it became a part of the new Women in Military Service for America Memorial*

And General Vaught commented that the wall seemed to be shabby, in disrepair, and incomplete.

The answer was that the hemicycle wall really meant nothing. It was designed in 1934 by the famous architectural firm of McKim, Mead, and White as part of an overall design of Memorial Drive and Memorial Bridge, which connected the Lincoln Memorial and Arlington National Cemetery. In the firm's plan the hemicycle would mark the end of Memorial Drive and signal the ceremonial entrance to Arlington National Cemetery. Charles Follen McKim had a deep love of classical Greek architecture, and the hemicycle wall was undoubtedly his idea.

But the wall had no symbolic meaning appropriate to the cemetery, and in time it became nothing more than a retaining wall holding back the soil of the cemetery, which inclined steeply toward Arlington House behind it. The hemicycle wall had been neglected, as its shabby appearance made quite evident.

And then General Vaught asked a startling question "Is the wall available?" she wanted to know. "Is the site available? Could the Women's Memorial be built there with the wall as a part of the memorial?"

In General Vaught's view the site was perfect. No location in all of Washington was more on the tourist path, and it had the connection with military history that she thought the Women's Memorial should have.

But how could the wall be available? Wasn't it a part of Arlington National Cemetery? Some inquiry turned up the little-known fact that the ceremonial wall actually was not a part of Arlington Cemetery. It was a part of the National Mall—indeed had been placed there to mark the official end of the Mall—and since the wall was not a part of the cemetery, it had been neglected over the years. The U.S. Army, which is responsible for the care and maintenance of Arlington National Cemetery, was not responsible for the wall. The

THE BEAUTY OF ARLINGTON NATIONAL CEMETERY *can be fully appreciated from the upper terrace of the Women's Memorial.*

National Park Service is responsible for other memorials and monuments on the Mall, such as the Vietnam Veterans Memorial, the Korean War Memorial, the Washington Monument, and many others. But because the wall seemed so much a part of the cemetery, the Park Service had long been reluctant to do anything with it.

So, after all, there might be one remaining site on the Mall, Washington's monumental axis, and General Vaught and her Women's Memorial board wanted it. National Park Service officials cautioned the board that even if use of the site might be approved, restoring the hemicycle wall could be very expensive. But after much discussion, the foundation board of directors became convinced that in restoring the site, it would be giving back to America a piece of its lost history. And what better place could there be to put the "lost history" of women's military contributions to the nation?

Convinced of the board's determination, the Park Service gave its complete support to the use of the site for the Women in Military Service for America Memorial. So well prepared was the board and so persuasive was General Vaught that, in an intensive six-week effort, approval was secured from the National Capitol Memorial Commission, the Commission on Fine Arts, and the National Capitol Planning Commission. On July 28, 1988, final approval came for the Women's Memorial to be built on the site of the ceremonial gateway to Arlington National Cemetery.

Never in the history of Washington, D.C., had approval to build a memorial on the National Mall been received so swiftly.

With the location of the Women's Memorial now approved, the foundation board engaged architects at Virginia Tech University to develop guidelines for a competition to design the memorial. Crucial information had to be given, clearly spelled out: the basic purpose of the memorial, the condition of the hemicycle wall, the kind of soil it was retaining, climatic conditions, and literally hundreds of other details. Aerial maps of the monumental corridor were prepared with instructions that the "view lines" from Memorial Bridge to Arlington National Cemetery and from Arlington House to the Kennedy grave site must not be interfered with. In other words, the Women's Memorial could not have any high spires or tower.

After the guidelines were prepared, a national design competition was announced, open to any American citizen. Over 130 designs were received from all over the country; in June 1989 they were reviewed by a panel of women veterans and distinguished architects and designers. They selected four finalists, and after a second round of selection the Women's Memorial Foundation announced the winner in November: the architectural team of Marion Gail Weiss and Michael Manfredi of New York City.

With the site selected and the design approved, the foundation board now began a huge campaign to raise the more than $20 million needed to build the memorial. A number of major U.S. corporations such as American Telephone and Telegraph (AT&T Corp.), General Motors Corp., and Continental Airlines made generous donations. The U.S. mint produced commemorative coins, the sale of which netted more than $3 million. Thirty state legislatures approved contributions, and thousands of private citizens sent money to help build the memorial. The building fund received a major boost from a federal grant of $9.5 million to be used only for the repair, restoration, and preservation of the main gate structures of Arlington National Cemetery. After more than five years of spirited campaigning the total amount needed to build the memorial was in hand.

The official groundbreaking ceremony was held on June 22, 1995. More than six thousand military women, active duty and veterans, came for the historic event. General Vaught, who officiated, noted that it was the largest gathering of servicewomen on record and that every state in the nation was represented. And she said, as she had said many times before, that the goal of all those who had worked for this day was to build

BRIGADIER GENERAL WILMA L. VAUGHT,
USAF (Ret.), presiding at the Women's Memorial ground-breaking ceremony

a memorial that would be more than just a statue. The goal was a memorial that would tell the story of women in military service for America and tell it in many ways.

President Bill Clinton was the main speaker and, in a tribute to General Vaught, said he was sure no one could have said no to her in her drive to make the Women's Memorial a reality. "I know I couldn't," he said.

The president then gave a moving tribute to women in the military. He reviewed their two centuries of contributions to the nation's defense and their determination to serve despite

PRESIDENT CLINTON AND GENERAL JOHN SHALIKASHVILI *greeting Anne Pedersen Freeman, one of the speakers at the groundbreaking ceremony. At the age of eighteen, Mrs. Freeman volunteered for service in the U.S. Navy during World War I. She was accepted and became a yeoman assigned to the Brooklyn Navy Yard. She told the audience that she didn't remember much about the mountains of navy forms she typed, but, in a sly dig at military red tape, she said, "I do remember that we made six copies of every-thing." Mrs. Freeman said she would have liked to serve longer in the navy but that all women except nurses were ter-minated within six months of the war's end. She also recalled that at the time she was in the navy, women in America did not have the right to vote.*

SHOVELS IN! *The leading dignitaries take part in the ceremonial groundbreaking for the new Women's Memorial.*

being treated as second-class soldiers. They could give their lives, he said, but they couldn't give orders to men. They could heal the wounded and hold the dying, but they couldn't dream of holding the highest ranks. They could take on the toughest assignments, but they couldn't take up arms. Still, they volunteered, fighting for freedom around the world but also fighting for the right to serve to the fullest of their potential. And from conflict to conflict, from Korea to Vietnam to the Persian Gulf, slowly women have overcome the barriers to their full service to America.

The president reviewed some important firsts that have taken place for women in the military in recent years: the first

West Point and Naval Academy graduates, the first female skipper of a Coast Guard vessel, the first woman fighter pilot. And then with a touch of pride he noted that during his administration the first woman had become head of one of the service branches: Secretary of the Air Force Sheila Widnall. With equal pride the president said that during his term of office 260,000 new positions in the military had been opened to women who wished to serve.

At the end of the ceremony shovels bit into the earth for the traditional ground breaking. The building of the Women in Military Service for America Memorial had begun.

Construction of the memorial took a little over two years. It was dedicated before an astonishing throng of more than 36,000 on October 18, 1997.

Three

A THOUSAND STORIES TO TELL

A thousand, of course, is only to scratch the surface. But the remarkable achievement of the Women in Military Service for America Memorial is in bringing together countless individual experiences—many unknown or little known until now—to tell the full story of how women, for more than two centuries, have served with and in American military forces to help defend their country.

The story is told in many ways: in hundreds of photographs in the exhibits; in the collections of uniforms, gear, and other materials relating to the lives of military women both overseas and on the home front; in films shown daily in the memorial theater; and in the computer registry that holds the records and experiences of more than 350,000 women who have served in the armed forces of the United States.

Women were not allowed to enlist in the Continental Army during the Revolutionary War, but women patriots found many ways to help the American cause. They passed

"VOLUNTEERING ON THE HOMEFRONT"

exhibit gives information about many of the civilian groups that worked with the military during World War II. The U.S. Cadet Nurse Corps was created by the U.S. Public Health Service because the country was not training enough nurses for both the war fronts and the home front. This very popular program produced more than 120,000 trained nurses.

information to the Continental Army, harbored patriot soldiers in safe houses, and stored arms and supplies for colonial troops. They worked for the Continental Army as cooks, laundresses, and water carriers. There are even accounts on record of women disguising themselves as men so they could fight with the colonial army on the battlefields.

The Women's Memorial makes especially clear the long, continuous presence of women as nurses with and in the

American armed forces. Even during the Revolutionary War the Continental Army medical corps was authorized to hire one female nurse for each ten sick or wounded soldiers.

Records of the War of 1812 are sparse, but ships' logs show that two female nurses, Mary Allen and Mary Marshall, were aboard Commodore Stephen Decatur's ship *United States* when it sailed on May 24, 1813. During the three-month siege of Fort Erie in 1814 the American defenders suffered over 1,800 casualties. Mary Ann Cole, working as a hospital matron, proved herself a true heroine as she cared for the wounded night and day, while at the same time preparing meals and keeping records for the regimental surgeon.

The Civil War brought dreadful casualties to both the Union and Confederate armies. Historians estimate that 10 percent of all soldiers between the ages of twenty and forty-nine died from wounds or injuries. In the desperate need for medical care the services of women were indispensable. Over 3,200 Northern women and over 1,000 Southern women served as civilian contract nurses. Catholic nuns were the only source of professionally trained nurses because there were no schools of nursing. Over 600 Catholic nuns became military nurses. The Sisters of Charity alone furnished 300 nurses and operated nineteen hospitals. During the war, Clara Barton nursed the wounded on the battlefields and became known as the Angel of the Battlefield. In 1864 she was appointed super-intendent of nurses for the Army of the James.

The Spanish-American War in 1898 was a war in which the American ground and naval forces crushed the Spanish enemy in Cuba and the Philippines with very few military casualties. Strangely, however, the need for nurses became acute and led to the recruiting of more than 1,500 civilian contract women nurses to work in army and navy hospitals in Cuba, the Philippines, and U.S. military camps. The problem there was tropical diseases. While only 400 men lost their lives

ON A GRASSY KNOLL IN A QUIET AND
PEACEFUL SECTION *of Arlington National Cemetery,
not far from the Women's Memorial, stands the Nurses
Memorial. The lovely white marble figure, erected in 1938
and rededicated in 1971, looks out over nearly a thousand
headstones of nurses of every service branch buried around her.
Nurses of every American war since the Spanish-American
War are here.*

in battle during this war, more than 4,500 were killed by yellow fever, malaria, and typhoid fever. Thousands more filled the military hospitals with these deadly diseases. Immune nurses—including thirty-two black nurses—who had already contracted and survived yellow fever, were assigned to the highest-risk hospitals in Cuba. The nurses worked valiantly in miserable conditions, with long hours, poor food, and inadequate living quarters. Their food often amounted to mush for breakfast and boiled cabbage and black coffee for dinner, but they stayed on the job and served even after the war ended. Twenty nurses died in service.

The critical need for nurses in time of war and the outstanding performance of civilian women nurses during the Spanish-American War led to the creation of the Army Nurse Corps in 1901 and the Navy Nurse Corps in 1908. With the creation of these two corps, women became official American military personnel for the first time in the nation's history.

The wisdom of having nurses readily available was quickly demonstrated when the army was called on to help in the San Francisco earthquake of 1906. It was America's entry into World War I in 1917, however, that showed why nurses needed to be an ever-ready part of the military. At the outset of the war, 466 navy nurses were ready for immediate duty. In the short, violent sixteen months that American troops fought in Europe, more than ten thousand nurses served overseas in field hospitals, mobile units, evacuation camps, and convalescent hospitals. They were also assigned to troop trains and transport ships. Another ten thousand army and navy nurses served in military hospitals in the United States. More than four hundred army, navy, and Red Cross nurses died overseas and in the United States during World War I. Most of these women died from an especially virulent form of influenza, which hit port cities and crowded military posts and hospitals especially hard.

During World War I women were for the first time enlisted in the military for positions other than nurses. Twelve thousand women served in the navy as yeomen, clerical workers in naval offices, in order to free men for duty at sea. At the end of the war, however, Congress closed loopholes that had allowed women to serve in the military except as nurses, and the army and navy nurse corps were reduced to their small prewar sizes.

THIS EXHIBIT *"Serving in the Military Since 1946" shows the wide range of activities of women in the military since World War II, in peacetime as well as in times of conflict: the Korean War, the Vietnam War, Panama, Operation Desert Storm, and Bosnia.*

World War I was supposed to be "the war to end all wars," but within twenty-five years the United States was at war again. On December 7, 1941, Japan attacked U.S. naval forces at Pearl Harbor in Hawaii, and the United States was immediately engulfed in World War II, fighting both in Europe and in the vastness of the Pacific. Women were needed in the military as never before, not only as nurses but in many other noncombatant roles such as ferrying airplanes, repairing military vehicles and weapons, and assuming thousands of desk jobs. All four military services formed women's components—army, navy, marines, Coast Guard—to serve "for the duration and six months." (The Air Force was not a separate service at that time.) Women also served in support of the military through the Red Cross, United Service Organization (USO), Cadet Nurse Corps, Civil Air Patrol, and in other ways.

During World War II military women served in all noncombatant areas in Europe, Africa, and the Pacific where U.S. forces were involved. And as is always the case, being in an area away from the front lines of action did not mean there was no danger. Sometimes what was a noncombatant area suddenly was not. Here is an experience that Janibell Smith, an army nurse in New Guinea, wrote to her mother about:

> Last night we had the worst air raid yet. It began around 9:00 p.m. when the sirens blew their warning. Every light was hastily extinguished—and then it began. The deafening reports of bombs, the artillery, the ack-ack coming from all directions, right over our heads—on one side of us a sudden flaming fire, the terrific sound of explosives—and then an enemy aircraft taking a sudden nose dive from the sky and zooming over us so closely that it brushed the tops of trees, so closely in fact that you could almost have shot down the pilot had you had an M-1 handy. Can you picture this happening again and again and again throughout the night? You run and stumble and fall in the darkness—

THIS EXHIBIT SHOWS HOW *the U.S. Army, Navy, Marines, and Coast Guard recruited and trained women and sent them out to work at field assignments. The navy's WAVES (Women Accepted for Volunteer Emergency Services) poster was one of the best-known World War II recruiting posters.*

sometimes you make the foxhole; mostly you just fling yourself flat in the sand and dust, wherever you happened to be. Next comes the sound of the ambulance siren—and you must forget everything except your helmet and your work.

Thirteen army nurses on a medical evacuation flight to Bari, Italy, in 1944 crashed in the mountains of Albania deep behind enemy lines. Germans were aware of the plane crash and searched for the survivors, even placing WANTED posters on trees. But the nurses and the plane crew evaded the German searchers, walked eight hundred miles across the mountains, and eventually reached the coast and freedom.

Of the hundreds of stories about World War II servicewomen, probably none tells more about their courage and determination than that of army nurse Lieutenant Deloris Buckley, a member of the 95th Evacuation Hospital. She was serving in North Africa when her unit was ordered to Italy where the Allies were fighting a major campaign. The hospital ship taking her unit to Italy was sunk by a Nazi dive-bomber. She managed to climb into one of the sinking ship's lifeboats, packed with other nurses and crew members, which was attempting to wend its way to the Italian shore, but shells from German and Italian guns drove them back to the open sea. There they were picked up by a U.S. destroyer and taken back to the North African port of Bizerte, Tunisia, from where they had started.

After a week the army decided it was safe enough for Lieutenant Buckley's lifeboat group to try again to reach Italy. This time they were transported in an LCI (Landing Craft Infantry). After a rough three days at sea, they landed at Paestum, a town between Naples and Salerno, which was now firmly in Allied hands. At Paestum they were reunited with the rest of their hospital unit personnel, who had survived in other lifeboats.

Lieutenant Buckley and her unit followed the advancing Allied troops, first working day and night in a hospital in Naples, then moving on to a place called Capua, where the casualties coming in to the field hospital were many and, as Lieutenant Buckley said, "I got my first real taste of the bloody business of war."

Remembering that time, Lieutenant Buckley said, "We were seasoned veterans. We had been through the thick of it at Capua, and there just wasn't anything worse."

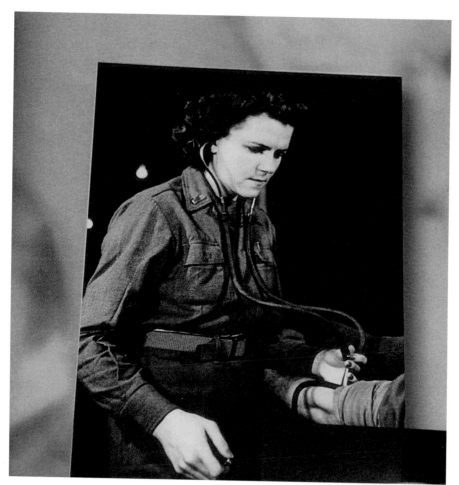

LIEUTENANT DELORIS BUCKLEY *was among the army nurses who served heroically in World War II.*

But she was wrong. Her unit was moved to Anzio, where the most savage fighting of the Italian campaign was taking place. Air bombardments came day and night. "The Nazis could not pinpoint their targets," Lieutenant Buckley said, "so they were just firing into a general area, and they had as much chance of hitting a Red Cross hospital as they had of landing on a legitimate military target."

And then one day it happened—Lieutenant Buckley remembers hearing a plane come in low: "There was a mighty roar that sounded as though the heavens had fallen down around my head. My whole body went numb. I remember thinking in a somewhat detached way that it was strange for me to be lying on the floor."

When Lieutenant Buckley did manage to get to her feet, she saw that she was covered with blood. She thought that an artery had been severed, but then she saw blood spurting through two holes in her thigh. A piece of shrapnel had entered through one side of her thigh and passed cleanly through the other. When she saw the total destruction that had hit the hospital, she clamped off her own bleeding veins and tried to help others. Six nurses died in the bombing.

Lieutenant Buckley and another wounded nurse were evacuated to a rest home in another part of Italy. Later their commanding colonel asked them if they wanted to be transferred back to the United States. They both said no—they wanted to go back to their evacuation hospital unit. "There was a real job waiting for us there," Lieutenant Buckley recounted, "and we would feel like quitters if we left now."

Among many remarkable stories of women's service on the home front in World War II, perhaps none is as remarkable as that of the Women Airforce Service Pilots, known to the entire country as WASPs. Early in the war the army saw the need to use women fliers for a number of crucial tasks in the United States that would free more men pilots for service overseas. The WASPs were civilians, but they were trained like military personnel and carried out many hazardous duties.

The army set up a training program at Avenger Field in Sweetwater, Texas. It was the only all-female military training base in the history of the U.S. military, and the conditions were tough. Just to be eligible to apply for training, a woman had to have a private pilot's license and at least thirty-five certified flying hours. If selected for training, the trainee had to pay her own way to Sweetwater. If at any time during the

THE COMPUTER REGISTRY *of the Women's Memorial has 350,000 entries such as this printout on Colonel Jacqueline O. Cochran.*

training she "washed out" (was eliminated), she had to pay her own way home. The training was for six months to learn to "fly the Army way." Two solo cross-country flights were required in training.

Despite the severe conditions, over 25,000 young women applied for training. Of that number 1,830 were accepted, and 1,074 successfully completed training. Why did so many young women accept the hard terms of WASP service? Years later Ms. F. G. Shutsy-Reynolds, an ex-WASP, summed it up this way: "We had some things in common: love of country, love of flying, desire to serve."

A GROUP OF WASPS *on their way to the skies*

And in a few words, Ms. Shutsy-Reynolds explained why that small group of women fliers has become an American legend:

Graduate WASPs were assigned to more than a hundred different bases in the United States. We flew more than sixty million miles in seventy-eight different types of military aircraft, ferrying them from the manufacturer to points of debarkation for overseas and operational squadrons. We flew war-weary aircraft to repair depots, instructed male pilots, and flew military aircraft on navigational training flights. The WASPs performed routine testing of military aircraft, flew administrative missions, towed targets for live gunnery practice, and in total flew every type mission except combat. So we couldn't shoot at the enemy, but it was okay to be shot at.

Having successfully achieved its goals of relieving male pilots for combat and proving that women were capable of flying military aircraft, the WASP program was disbanded in December 1944. During the program's lifetime thirty-eight WASP pilots were killed in the line of duty. An unhappy commentary on government's lack of concern for women in the military at that time in our nation's history is that WASPs served without the usual military benefits. If a WASP was killed in the performance of her duty, there was no insurance or burial expenses—everything had to be taken care of by family or friends.

But this pioneering program in women's aviation far exceeded what had been expected of it. In a moving tribute General Henry "Hap" H. Arnold, Commander of the U.S. Army Air Force during World War II, said: "...the WASPs proved they could fly wing tip to wing tip with their brothers in the sky at a time of critical need in our country." Without question the WASPs paved the way for and were role models for the women U.S. Air Force pilots of today.

Many years after World War II, the WASPs were finally recognized by the federal government as a part of the U.S. military. As Ms. Shutsy-Reynolds wrote, "Finally, WASP were issued honorable discharges and medals. All benefits had run out years ago except one—now we can have a flag on our coffin."

In photographs, films, and computer registry the Women's Memorial records the progress of African-American women in the military. Historical records show that free or recently freed black women worked as civilian nurses for the Union army and navy during the Civil War. Five black nurses served under the direction of Catholic nuns aboard the famous navy hospital ship *Red Rover*. As many as 180 black nurses served in U.S. government hospitals in several states. Susie King Taylor, freed from slavery by Union forces, became a nurse and laundress for the First South Carolina Volunteers, an all-black unit created by Union officers. Able to read and write, Mrs. King Taylor also set up a school for black children and soldiers who had never had any schooling. Mrs. King Taylor later wrote a book about her experiences, *A Black Woman's Civil War Memoirs.*

Although many African-American nurses wanted to serve in World War I, only a few were finally accepted into the Army Nurse Corps. They were assigned to care for black soldiers and German prisoners of war and lived in segregated quarters. During World War II more than 6,500 African-American women served in the Women's Army Corps (WAC). Many more would have served, but recruitment of black women was limited to 10 percent of the total WAC strength. The African-American WACs were dubbed "ten-percenters." They participated in segregated training and served in segregated units. The navy barred African-American women from the WAVES until late in the war and then accepted only a few enlistments.

After World War II, on July 26, 1948, President Harry S. Truman courageously issued Executive Order 9981, which eliminated racial segregation, quotas, and discrimination in all U.S. military services. At first, some military leaders were reluctant to implement the president's order, arguing that the military was not the place to try out "social experiments." A stubborn, determined man, President Truman kept the pressure for change on the military. Six years after Executive Order 9981, the Department of Defense announced that segregation had been eliminated in all of the armed services. From that time on, discrimination was not officially tolerated in the U.S. military.

These official changes and the great social breakthroughs in civil rights in the 1960s have led to greatly increased participation by African-American women in all the military services. Many served with distinction during the Vietnam War.

FIRST SERGEANT AGATHA W. DAVIS, *U.S. Army (center), at her 1974 retirement ceremony. She was first sergeant of an all-male student officer group at Aberdeen Proving Ground, Maryland. With her at the retirement ceremony are her husband, Sergeant Major James Davis, and their daughter, Brenda.*

Major Marie L. Rogers of the Army Nurse Corps received the Bronze Star from President Lyndon Johnson in a White House ceremony in December 1967. The medal was given for her operating-room heroism during action against the enemy. Army nurse Diane M. Lindsay, 95th Evacuation Hospital, Vietnam, received the Soldier's Medal for heroism. She was the first black nurse to receive the award and was promoted to captain. Many important "firsts" continue for African-American servicewomen. In 1995, Brigadier General Marcelite Harris, USAF, was promoted to major general, the first black woman to attain that rank. In 1997, Army Sergeant Danyell Wilson became the first black woman to earn the prestigious assignment of guarding the Tomb of the Unknowns at Arlington National Cemetery.

What is perhaps most remarkable about African-American women in the military today, though, is a simple statistic: Almost half—48 percent—of all enlisted women in the U.S. Army are now African Americans. Twenty percent of all women officers in the army are African Americans. The percentage of African-American enlisted women in the marines, navy, and air force is double that of the percentage of African Americans in the general population (12 percent).

These remarkably high percentages of peacetime enlistment are clear evidence that African-American women see career and educational opportunities in military service that are perhaps less available in civilian life. Training and experience gained in the military often can be a stepping stone for all women to later employment in civilian life.

How many stories does the Women in Military Service for America Memorial have to tell? Too many to count, but as General Vaught has said, all have been brought together as a gift to the American people.

Four

BEYOND THE YEAR 2000: STORIES YET TO BE TOLD

The determination of American women to win the right to serve in the military forces of the United States in defense of the nation has never wavered. World Wars I and II made clear the vital need for women in the military in times of national emergency, but it was not until 1948 that the Women's Armed Services Integration Act granted women perma-nent status in the regular and reserve forces of the army, navy, marine corps and the newly created, separate air force.

Even then the number of women in the armed forces was limited to 2 percent, and ceilings on women's promotions kept them out of the ranks of general and admiral. It was not until 1967 that President Lyndon Johnson signed a law repealing the highly discriminatory ceiling on women's promotions and dropping the 2 percent limit on both officer and enlisted strengths for women in the armed forces.

In 1975, President Gerald Ford signed Public Law 94-106 admitting women to the military academies. Women were

51

TAKEN FROM THE COMPUTER REGISTRY, *this printout gives detailed information about the service record of Lieutenant General Carol A. Mutter, USMC, who served in the Vietnam War and in Operation Desert Storm.*

enrolled in all service academies by the fall of 1976. Just eight years later, in 1984, Kristine Holderied graduated at the top of her class at the U.S. Naval Academy in Annapolis, Maryland.

In many other ways military women pushed on. In 1970, Anna Mae Hays, Chief, Army Nurse Corps, and Elizabeth P. Hoisington, Director of the Women's Army Corps, became the first women promoted to general. In 1973, six navy women were the first women to earn military pilot wings. Army Lieutenant Sally Murphy became the first military helicopter pilot

LIEUTENANT COMMANDER CHARLOTTE HUNTER *was commissioned an ensign in the navy in 1986 and became a chaplain after attending the eight-week chaplains school.*

She has been a chaplain in a number of naval and marine stations, including the naval support facility on the tiny island of Diego Garcia in the Indian Ocean. She was stationed in Camp Pendleton, California, when the Gulf War started and wanted to go to Saudi Arabia but thought there was no chance. On a trip to Washington she went to see the Marine Corps chaplain to plead her case. When she entered his office, he was on the phone, and he looked up in amazement. "Charlotte," he said, "I was trying to reach you in Camp Pendleton. You are being assigned to Saudi Arabia." Lieutenant Commander Hunter went to Saudi Arabia, assigned to Headquarters of the 3rd Marine Air Wing, in January 1991 and stayed until well after hostilities ended in Kuwait. She is now assigned as a teacher at the Naval Chaplains School in Newport, Rhode Island.

in 1974. That same year the Department of Defense changed its policy to permit women to remain in the military while raising families. In 1983, Lieutenant Colleen Nevius became the navy's first woman test pilot.

Despite these gains and many others like them, laws and policies continued to restrict women in the military to non-combatant areas and to bar them from flying in combat and serving aboard combat ships. Those jobs and assignments continued to be for men only.

Then in 1991 came Operation Desert Storm, the short, ferocious Persian Gulf War that the United States fought against Iraq in the Arabian Peninsula. Approximately 41,000 military women were among the troops deployed to Saudi Arabia and Kuwait, the small, oil-rich country that Iraq invaded. Never before in United States history had so many women in the armed forces been assigned so close to a combat area. As Washington Post correspondent Molly Moore wrote, "On this desert battlefield, with its long-range missiles and high-technology weaponry, the front lines were so blurred that the combat-exclusion laws were virtually meaningless."

Thousands of women soldiers and marines were closer to the combat zone than many of their male counterparts. And they did everything the men did. They drove trucks, ferried airplanes, repaired tanks, operated communications equipment, stood guard duty, carried guns, and shouldered much of the burden in field hospitals. Two women were taken prisoners of war, and five were killed in action.

One of those taken prisoner was Major (now Lieutenant Colonel) Rhonda Cornum, an Army Medical Corps physician. She was on a search and rescue mission when the Black Hawk helicopter she was in was shot down by intensive Iraqi antiaircraft fire. Five of the persons in the Black Hawk were killed instantly when it crashed, while three others, including Major

UNITED STATES SERVICEWOMEN *in Operation*
Desert Storm

Cornum, were taken prisoner by Saddam Hussein's elite
Republican Guard. Major Cornum suffered two broken arms,
a smashed knee, and a bullet wound. After her release, Major
Cornum was sent to Walter Reed Medical Center in Wash-
ington, D.C., for convalescence. She received the Purple
Heart, Distinguished Flying Cross, and the Joint Chiefs of
Staff Award for Excellence in Military Medicine, which she is
most proud of.

A belief of Colonel Cornum's about women in the military is
etched into one of the glass skylights on the terrace of the
Women's Memorial. It is this:

The qualities that are most important in all military jobs—things like integrity, moral courage, and determination—have nothing to do with gender.

More and more the lawmakers in Congress and the policy makers in the armed forces are agreeing that most military restrictions based solely on whether a person is a man or a woman do not make sense. In 1992, Congress repealed laws

COLONEL EILEEN M. COLLINS *became the first woman commander of a space shuttle, Columbia, in July 1999*

MANY SCHOOL GROUPS ON FIELD TRIPS *to Washington schedule a visit to the Women's Memorial.*

banning women from flying in combat. In 1993, Congress repealed the ban on women serving aboard combat ships. The only major combat exclusion now remaining is the one prohibiting women from serving in ground combat, where greater physical strength than most women have is necessary.

The struggle of women to find their rightful place in the military has never been about proving that they can do anything men can do. It has been about having the chance to make their place in their branch of service based on their ability rather than on gender.

As retired Air Force Major General Jeanne Holm states in her epic book *Women in the Military: An Unfinished Revolution*, the goal of women in the military is to secure that right to accept the challenge of the recruiting poster: *Be All That You Can Be*.

The Women in Military Service for America Memorial will tell the stories of the future as women continue to show the country "all that they can be."

Information about the WOMEN IN MILITARY SERVICE FOR AMERICA MEMORIAL

Hours of the memorial's operation:
8 A.M. to 5 P.M., October 1 to March 31
8 A.M. to 7 P.M., April 1 to September 30

Open every day except Christmas
Memorial Internet address:
wimsa@aol.com

Memorial World Wide Web site:
www.wimsa.org

Those interested in learning more about the Women in Military Service for America Memorial should contact the Women's Memorial Foundation as specified below:

Address: Department 560
                Arlington, Virginia 22204

Telephone: (800) 222-2294

FAX: (703) 931-4208

Bibliography

Ashabranner, Brent. *Their Names to Live: What the Vietnam Veterans Memorial Means to America.* New York: Twenty-First Century Books, 1998.

Bellafaire, Judith. "Women in Military Service for America Memorial." Women's Memorial information release, 1998.

Conklin, Eileen. *Women at Gettysburg.* Gettysburg, PA: Thomas Publications, 1993.

David, Peter. *Triumph in the Desert.* New York: Random House, 1991.

Friedl, Vicki. *Women in the U.S. Military 1901–1995.* Westport, CT: Greenwood Press, 1996.

Holm, Jeanne. *Women in the Military: An Unfinished Revolution.* (Revised edition.) Novato, CA: Presidio Press, 1992.

———. *In Defense of a Nation: Servicewomen in World War II.* Arlington, VA: Vandamere Press, 1998.

Moore, Molly. *A Woman at War.* New York: Charles Scribner's Sons, 1993.

Norman, Elizabeth. *Women at War.* Philadelphia: University of Pennsylvania Press, 1990.

Saywell, Shelley. *Women in War: First-Hand Accounts from World War II to El Salvador*. New York: Viking Press, 1985.

Sheldon, Kathryn. "Women in Military Service for America." Women's Memorial release, 1998.

Taylor, Susie King. *A Black Woman's Civil War Memoirs*. Princeton, NJ: Markus Wiener Publishers, 1988.

Index

Page numbers in *italics* refer to illustrations.